Bullying

DEBORAH CHANCELLOR

W

FRANKLIN WATTS

LONDON • SYDNEY

First published in 2009
by Franklin Watts

Copyright © Franklin Watts 2009

Franklin Watts
338 Euston Road
London NW1 3BH

Franklin Watts Australia
Level 17/207 Kent Street
Sydney, NSW 2000

Series editor: Sarah Peutrill
Editor: Sarah Ridley
Art director: Jonathan Hair
Design: www.rawshock.co.uk
Picture research: Diana Morris

Dewey number: 302.3'4

ISBN 978 0 7496 8830 1

Printed in Malaysia

Franklin Watts is a division of Hachette
Children's Books, an Hachette UK company.
www.hachette.co.uk

Picture credits: Paul Baldesare/Photofusion: 12.
John Birdsall/PA Photos: 13, 14, 17. Chapman/
Wiedelphoto/Photofusion: 22. Robert
Churchill/istockphoto: 10. Damir Cudic/
istockphoto: 19. Mikael Damkiev/istockphoto: 1,
5. Digital Vision/Getty Images: front cover, 6.
Randy Farls/Corbis: 21. Matt Matthews/
istockphoto: 23. Roy McMahon/
Corbis: 18. Gideon Mendel/Corbis: 11.
Jonathan Meyers/Alamy: 29. Greg
Nicholas/istockphoto: 25. Jose Luis
Pelaez/Corbis: 8. Margot Petrowski/Fotofolia:
27. John Powell/Photofusion: 4. Paula
Solloway/Photofusion: 9, 16. Nikolay
Titov/istockphoto: 15. Bob Watkins/
Photofusion: 28. Janine Wiedel/Photofusion:
26. Zilli/istockphoto: 24. Some photos have
been posed by models. Every attempt has been
made to clear copyright. Should there be any
inadvertent omission please apply to the
publisher for rectification.

CONTENTS

Look out for these features

A more detailed information panel.

An opportunity to get together with some friends and each take a point of view and follow it through.

An invitation to explore your own feelings.

DILEMMA
Focus on someone's difficult decision and think how you might advise them.

Look at both sides of the argument and see which you agree with.

Some topics that you could research yourself, either in the library or on the Internet.

What is bullying?

Bullying is unkind behaviour towards someone that occurs several times. It can happen to anyone at any age. Whilst some people are bullied by their brothers or sisters, others are bullied by other children, adults or employers. We all need to face up to the problem of bullying, and think about what can be done to prevent it.

Constantly leaving someone out and encouraging others to ignore them is a form of bullying.

Different types of bullying

Bullying can take several different forms.

- Physical bullying is hitting, kicking, pinching and pushing.
- Verbal bullying is spoken or written insults.
- Emotional bullying involves using threatening behaviour, leaving someone out constantly, or making someone feel humiliated and useless.

In all cases, the bullying behaviour has to happen more than once to count as bullying. Many bullies pick on the same person over and over again.

One or more

Some bullies act alone, others gain power by acting as a group. Bullies are not always big and strong — they may be clever and sly, and able to control other people. When bullies belong to a group it can make them feel less responsible for their bad behaviour.

Bullying may make people feel unhappy, worried, scared and alone.

What's wrong with bullying?

People who are bullied often feel lonely and powerless. This makes them stressed and sad, and can even lead to depression. They may start to feel bad about themselves. Often people find it hard to study, especially if they start to skip school to avoid the bully. In extreme cases, bullying has led to suicide.

Signs of bullying

If someone is being bullied, their behaviour may change, for example they may stop eating properly or start skipping school. Some people become moody, ill or cannot sleep properly. Unexplained cuts, bruises and torn clothes can be a sign. However, all these things also happen for other reasons.

IN FOCUS

Bullying in primary school
A quarter of all primary school pupils are bullied at least once a term. They are more than twice as likely to be bullied as older children.

? Dilemma:

Tammy's best friend Sonia makes fun of a girl in their class because her trainers are old-fashioned. The girl accuses Sonia of being a bully, but Sonia says she is only joking. Who is right? Should Tammy say anything to Sonia?

Why do people bully?

People become bullies for many reasons. Some people feel unhappy about themselves and take it out on other people by bullying them. Others may be prejudiced about something, for example a particular race or religion.

Some children bully to get attention, become popular or to feel 'big' in front of their friends.

Bully or victim?

There is never an excuse for bullying, but research shows that bullies have often been treated badly by other people. In the UK, one in five bullies has been bullied in the past. They often have low self-esteem, which means they don't feel good about themselves, however confident they may seem. Some bullies have seen or experienced violence in the home, either from carers or siblings.

Understanding behaviour

Bullies might have no idea how much their behaviour is hurting someone else. They may not even realise that they have turned into a bully. Once someone has understood that he or she has been bullying another person, they must always apologise to the victim.

Once a bully, always a bully?

In the US, research shows that about a quarter of school bullies gain a criminal record by the time they are 30. While some people believe that bullies can't change their ways, others believe that if bullies are challenged in the right way, they will understand what they have done, learn what is acceptable and then change their behaviour.

Do you think you should try to understand and help bullies, or simply condemn them for the harm they do?

IN FOCUS

Prejudice

Prejudice is having an opinion, a like or dislike about something, without really knowing the true facts about it. Prejudice often leads to unfair and unkind treatment of another person. Some people are prejudiced about disability, others about physical size or race.

ARGUMENTS FOR AND AGAINST PUNISHING BULLIES

FOR!

AGAINST!

- There is no excuse for bullying. Bullies leave victims damaged, emotionally and physically, and this damage can last a lifetime. They should be made to pay for this.
- If bullies aren't punished, they will think they have got away with their behaviour. They may grow up thinking that using violence and threats to get what you want is acceptable.

- Many bullies have been bullied themselves, and see bullying as 'acceptable'. Punishment won't make them understand why they should stop.
- Bullies need to be helped to understand what they have done so they can change for the better. Punishment won't make this happen.

Emotional bullying

Emotional bullying can involve threats, but it may not be as obvious as that. Much emotional bullying isolates the victim by ignoring them, leaving them out of the group, or forcing others not to be friends with them. Spiteful behaviour like this makes the victim feel anxious and unhappy, and perhaps even makes them blame themselves for what is going on.

Being unfriendly

Emotional bullies may be mean or unfriendly to their victims, or they may not let them join in with fun activities. They use threats, like saying they will spread rumours, so they can get what they want.

Only joking?

Bullies often make excuses for themselves by saying that they are 'only joking'. But taunting or tormenting someone is a form of bullying even if the threats are never carried out. Although no words are spoken, making threatening gestures or pulling horrible faces is also bullying.

Cruelly making fun of other children is a form of bullying.

Bullies often pick on children who have just joined a school, because they are new and different.

Damage and theft

Tormenting someone by constantly stealing their books, school bag, lunchbox or mobile phone is another form of emotional bullying. Even if the goods are returned to the owner, it causes anxiety and fear to the victim of the bullying.

YOUR CALL There is a new girl in your class. People are not letting her join in their games at playtime, and are being unfriendly towards her. What could you do?

ROLE PLAY: ARE SOME KINDS OF BULLYING WORSE THAN OTHERS?

These two people disagree about bullying. Who do you think is right?

1 "Physical bullying is worse than emotional or verbal bullying, because violence can hurt and even kill people."

Nurse, Phil Jones

2 "All kinds of bullying are wrong because they make people feel bad about themselves. Any kind of bullying can lead to problems to do with the mind."

Counsellor, Ben Sims

? Dilemma:
Abdul is unhappy at work because his boss keeps criticising him in front of everyone in the office. Should he put up with this emotional bullying, or complain and risk losing his job?

Verbal bullying

U nkind words can be just as damaging as spiteful actions. Nasty remarks or constant criticism make people's lives a misery. Verbal bullying takes many forms, but it includes teasing, name-calling, sarcastic remarks, gossiping and spreading rumours. This kind of bullying is often, but not always, carried out by girls.

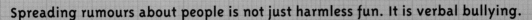
Spreading rumours about people is not just harmless fun. It is verbal bullying.

Picking on differences

Some people are bullied for no particular reason, but bullies sometimes make fun of people who stand out from the crowd. They may pick on a difference they can't understand, or feel threatened by.

People who have special needs or learning difficulties, or even extremely clever people, are sometimes picked on by bullies. Just not quite 'fitting in' to a particular situation or school, can bring people to the attention of a bully.

An autistic child joins in with a tug-of-war competition. Many schools work hard to include all their pupils in activities.

Do you think there would be less verbal bullying in schools if children were taught more about issues such as disability? Or would this make the bullying even worse?

RESEARCH IT YOURSELF

Find out about issues that people are bullied for such as autism, dyslexia or obesity.

Written abuse

Poison pen letters, insulting graffiti and other forms of written abuse are all verbal bullying. They are targeted at individuals, in order to frighten and upset them. Although these actions leave strong evidence of bullying, it can be hard to discover who wrote the words. Police may be asked to investigate serious cases of written abuse.

Sexual bullying

Unwanted comments on someone's appearance or attractiveness are a form of bullying. Calling a person 'gay' as a put-down, meaning that they are not very good at something, is also unacceptable. Giving someone unwanted physical attention, such as hugging or bottom-pinching, is sexual bullying.

? Dilemma:

Lewis and Alfie are 13 years old, and are good friends. Someone at their school starts a rumour that they are gay. What do you think they should do? Should they ignore the rumour, or speak to a teacher about it? Homophobic bullying is a growing problem among young people and adults, and, unlike racist bullying, there is no law against it.

Physical bullying

A ny repeated use of violence towards someone, such as pushing, kicking, hitting or punching, is physical bullying. It can be very frightening and dangerous. It is important not to ignore any signs or evidence of physical bullying, for example unexplained bruises or cuts. The person who is being bullied may really need help.

Physical bullying is a very frightening experience for the victim.

Gang bullying

Gang members gain strength from acting together. Picking on one child gives them a joint purpose and draws them closer as a group. It is never acceptable to hurt anyone else, whether in a one-off fight, or by constant bullying. In fact, if a child is injured in a bullying attack, the bullies or bully could be arrested for causing 'actual bodily harm' — see IN FOCUS box, opposite.

Boys or girls?

In the past, physical bullying was usually only carried out by boys, and boys are often still involved in this type of bullying. However, some girls are becoming more assertive and aggressive. Now there is a greater chance that girls will take part in acts of physical bullying.

Happy slapping

'Happy slapping' has nothing to do with being happy. It is when a case of physical bullying is recorded on a mobile phone and then sent to other people, to show off about it. The victim is hurt twice over — once by the actual attack and then by the humiliation of many people watching the attack.

For safety's sake, sometimes the best thing is to run away from bullies, but tell an adult afterwards to stop it from happening again.

? Dilemma:
Josh is being physically bullied on the way home from school, but is too scared to talk about it. His mum asks him how he got his bruises and tore his shirt. The bullies have threatened him with worse if he tells on them. What should he do?

IN FOCUS

Actual bodily harm

Certain types of bullying are against the law. If physical bullying leads to cuts, bruises, broken bones or other injuries, this is called actual bodily harm (ABH). The police may be called in to investigate. A teenager found guilty of actual bodily harm can be excluded from their school, and may be given a sentence, such as community work, by a court.

YOUR CALL Some people think the way to stop children hurting other children is to punish the parents. Do you think this would work, or do you think it is the bullies themselves who should be punished? Who is really responsible?

Cyber bullying

Today, most of us use computers and mobile phones every day. These new forms of communication have given rise to a different type of bullying called cyber bullying. It can take a variety of forms, from picking on someone in a chat room, to sending out nasty emails or text messages, setting up abusive websites, or posting unpleasant remarks on Internet message boards.

Mobile phones

A mobile phone can be a useful weapon for a bully. Threatening or silent calls are frightening, as are abusive text messages. A recent study showed that over a third of all children with mobile phones have received name-calling texts.

Internet bullying

Anyone can post abuse on an Internet message board, or set up a nasty website about someone. It is possible to get sites like this taken down, and messages can be deleted, if the right action is taken. The charity Bullying UK (see page 31) can help victims of cyber bullying sort out this kind of problem.

Bullies can reach their victims easily on a mobile phone.

YOUR CALL If you received nasty calls on your mobile phone, would you get a new phone and change your number, or is that letting the bully win?

? Dilemma:
Graham is a teacher. His job has become unbearable since his name and photo appeared on an abusive website, with insulting comments about him. Many of his pupils have visited the website. What should he do?

It is important to keep safe on the Internet, especially if you are using chat rooms.

INTERNET DO'S AND DON'TS

DO!

DON'T!

DO tell an adult if someone online makes worrying suggestions to you.

DO take an adult friend or parent with you to meet a new friend you have made online.

DO use a pin code on your phone so that only you can use it.

DO keep copies of any abusive texts or messages and **DO** show them to an adult who will help you to solve the problem.

DO use the security settings on any chat room websites, so that only the people you list can chat with you.

DON'T give your real name, address or phone number to anyone online.

DON'T say where you go to school or give out details of your family to anyone online.

DON'T agree to meet up with anyone you meet online on your own.

DON'T post photos or information about other people, or yourself, that others might use against you or them.

Racist bullying

Racist bullying is when a bully repeatedly picks on someone because of the colour of their skin, their religion or culture. The bully will often make insulting remarks about the person's family or way of life. This type of bullying can take any form, verbal, emotional or physical. It can include taunts, graffiti and gestures. It may involve leaving a person out of an activity, or refusing to play or work with them.

Why does it happen?

Racist bullying happens when people are prejudiced about colour, race, religion or culture. Some children hear their parents' racist views at home and absorb them as they grow up. This might make them feel it is acceptable to pick on racial differences, such as making fun of a Sikh boy for wearing a turban.

It is wrong to pick on people just because they wear different clothes or hairstyles.

Racist graffiti is a form of racist bullying. Racist bullying in schools must be recorded, by law. This graffiti in Spain is by a group who have racist views about Jewish people.

Take action

If racist bullying happens inside or outside a school, anyone who sees it must tell a teacher or another adult. It is not an option to do nothing. This will allow the racist bullying to continue, and means the person who saw the incident becomes involved in the racism. The law states that schools must record all instances of racist bullying.

IN FOCUS
Racism

Racism is treating someone differently because they belong to a different race or culture. It also refers to treating people unfairly because of their religion or nationality. Racism is against the law in many countries, including the UK and Australia.

ROLE-PLAY: CULTURE CLASH

These people have different views on how people should be treated. Who do you agree with and why?

1 "If people are different to you, and live their lives in a different way, you can't treat them the same as people who are exactly like you."

Accountant, Jo Smith

2 "No two people are the same, whatever their race or cultural background. But we all have the right to be treated in the same way."

Vicar, Rev. Paul Glister

Bullying at Home

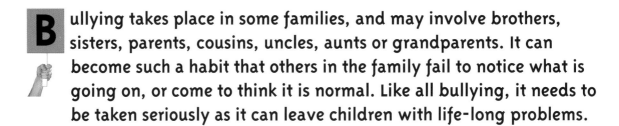

Bullying takes place in some families, and may involve brothers, sisters, parents, cousins, uncles, aunts or grandparents. It can become such a habit that others in the family fail to notice what is going on, or come to think it is normal. Like all bullying, it needs to be taken seriously as it can leave children with life-long problems.

In the family

Parents do not always know that one of their children is bullying another. They may think that a real problem of bullying is just a case of brothers and sisters arguing, or being jealous of each other. The bullied child could talk to another family member such as a grandparent, or a trusted friend, to help sort things out.

New families

When parents split up and begin new relationships, children have to get used to step-brothers and sisters or even a new baby. Some children feel threatened, insecure or unhappy when this happens, and may take this out on their new brothers and sisters. Often life settles down again, but if the bullying continues, the bullied child should seek help.

It is natural for children to argue sometimes, but parents don't always realise when it has turned into bullying.

Parent trouble

Children who are being bullied by a parent may not know who to talk to. Often the bullying takes the form of constant nagging or criticism that makes the child lose confidence. The child can feel isolated and fear that no one will take them seriously or believe what they say. Or they may think that things will get worse if they speak out about what is happening to them. Children in this situation could ring Childline in the UK (see page 31).

The telephone can be a lifeline to children who are being bullied at home.

IN FOCUS
Child abuse

Bullying at home may turn into child abuse. This can have lifelong effects on the victim, leaving them with physical or mental scars. Child abuse of any sort must be stopped. Several organisations, including the NSPCC, Childline and Kidscape, work hard to help children who are being abused — see page 31 for contact details.

ROLE PLAY: BROTHERLY LOVE?

Families may disagree about how to deal with bullying. Who do you think is right in this situation?

1 "My brother Connor is older, bigger and stronger than me. He taunts and threatens me at home, but Mum doesn't believe me when I tell her about it. She always sides with Connor, no matter what I say."

11-year-old, Callum Brown

2 "All brothers argue – it's normal. There's nothing unusual about Connor's behaviour. Callum should stop telling tales and grow up."

Callum and Connor's mother, Kate Brown

Bullying at school

Bullying can happen in any kind of school, state or private, and between children of any age. It may happen in the playground, in toilets, in changing rooms, corridors and classrooms — usually out of adults' sight. It is not a new problem, but it always needs to be taken seriously.

School gangs

Many children are in a gang at school — it is just a group of friends who enjoy being together. Sometimes gangs decide to use their joint strength to bully people. Even if a gang member does not actually do any of the bullying, he or she is still involved because he or she is not doing anything to stop it. Bullying can make some children's schooldays a misery, so it needs to be stopped.

Facing the problem

Schools have different ways of dealing with bullying.
- 'Friendship' benches — somewhere safe where children go to talk to someone.
- 'Bullying boxes' — where children leave messages about bullying for teachers to act on.
- 'Peer support' — where a bullied child can talk to someone their own age, who has been given some training. The peer support child will have ideas about how to solve problems between students.
- 'Bullying courts' — where children and teachers discuss problems.

Are you a school bully?

Some school pupils can be bullies without realising it — they think they are just having fun with their friends, but someone else might not see it that way.

Is your teacher a bully?

Adults can be bullies as well as children. While it is rare for teachers to be bullies, some teachers pick on pupils in an unfair way, and action should be taken to stop this. Talk to your parents about it.

? Dilemma:
Hannah is being bullied on her way to and from school, on the school bus. The bus driver never seems to notice. Who should she ask for help — her school, her parents or the bus company?

YOUR CALL Do you think 'bullying boxes' are a good idea, or do they give children a chance to lie about people they don't like?

For some children, the journey to school is the worst part of the day.

ROLE-PLAY: FOR AND AGAINST MOVING SCHOOLS

Sometimes a child changes schools to get away from bad bullying. Follow these arguments through.

1

"It was dangerous for my child to stay where he was. A fresh start will give him the chance to make new friends."

Parent, Anna Preet

2

"Bullies are in all schools, so they are impossible to avoid. The new school may be worse than the old one."

Headteacher, David Johnson

Bullying in Sport

In sport, bullying can take place on and off the pitch. Sometimes team mates bully each other during the game or in the changing room. It is also possible for a coach to bully members of the team, or for pushy parents to bully their own children.

A good coach will bring out the best in the team.

Who is to blame?

Sometimes a coach can become so focused on winning that he or she may bully team members, in an effort to make them perform better. The coach is in a position of power and should lead young people by setting a good example. It is easy to destroy a person's confidence through constant criticism. Even if bad sporting mistakes have been made, it is unfair and humiliating to always blame one person.

? Dilemma:
Jamal's rugby coach has favourites, but bullies some members of the team. Jamal loves rugby, and doesn't want to lose his place in the squad. Should he blow the whistle on his coach, and tell someone at the rugby club?

Children can be put under a lot of pressure when they play sport.

YOUR CALL Are 'pushy parents' better than parents who don't go to watch their children play sports? Why or why not?

ROLE-PLAY: HIGH EXPECTATIONS...

These people disagree on what is important about sport. Who do you agree with?

1 "Sports should be competitive and children should play to win. The most important thing is the result of the match."

Parent, Jack MacBride

2 "The most important thing is to enjoy taking part in sport. Some parents are too pushy, and put too much pressure on their children."

Coach, Peter Skinner

Pushy parents

Parents should set a good example to their children. Whilst it is good to encourage children to succeed in sport, some parents put too much pressure on their children to win. They may criticise their children if they don't perform well, bullying them verbally. They may also threaten other adults who are involved in the sport, including the referees or the coach. Clubs sometimes ban parents like this from attending matches.

Team players

Learning how to work in a team is a good result of playing team sport. Unfortunately, some people turn into bullies within their own team. They may pick on a child from a different background or on someone who stands out from the crowd.

Stop the bullying!

No one deserves to be bullied. Bullying can make people feel so frightened that they don't want to talk about it. Bullying is always wrong, so it is very important for victims of bullying to get help.

Tell someone

The bullying won't stop if no one knows it is happening. A bullied child should tell someone about it — maybe a relative, a trusted friend, a teacher or a school nurse. There are also helplines that people can phone for advice — see page 31. For five years running, bullying has been the most common reason that children have called the UK charity Childline.

Keep a record

Try keeping a record of everything the bully does or says, and a note of when and where it happens. This could mean writing down what happens, drawing pictures or making a video diary. Evidence will help other people to deal with the problem.

Keep calm

Bullies are looking for a reaction. If they don't get one, they may give up. So, try walking away from the situation and not answering back. If you fight back, it will make it difficult for any adult to sort out who is in the wrong.

It is helpful to keep a record of everything a bully says or does.

Gain confidence

If someone is bullied, it can be hard to feel positive about anything. However, it is important to focus on good things, such as a pet or a favourite hobby. In this way, the bullying doesn't take over. Some people join martial arts classes as it makes them feel more confident. Others practise a quick put-down response at home, to be ready the next time they are bullied.

Avoid danger

Learn to avoid the places where the bullying normally takes place. Make sure you have got your friends around most of the time. Don't take risks — run away fast if you think you are in danger, or hand over your lunch money, for instance, if you feel that you are about to be hurt. However, always tell an adult about the incident so that they can help sort out the problem.

Some victims of bullying learn self-defence, for example judo, to feel safe.

ROLE-PLAY: COPING WITH BULLYING

These two children have different ways of coping with bullying. Who do you agree with?

1 "Keep out of the bully's way, and don't grass them up, because that will get you in even worse trouble than before."

Pupil, Kayleigh Hampton

2 "Talk to somebody about your problem, don't keep it all to yourself. If you don't say anything, things will only get worse."

Pupil, Ali Hussein

RESEARCH IT YOURSELF

Find out about anti-bullying organisations. Start with these websites: www.bullying.co.uk; www.antibullying.net; www.childline.org.uk; www.kidscape.org.uk; www.nspcc.org.uk.

 If you were being bullied, would you stay at home to avoid the bully, or tell an adult about it?

When people witness a bullying incident, it can make them feel helpless and convinced that nothing can be done about the problem. However, it is possible to stand up to bullies and challenge their behaviour. Doing and saying nothing will simply give the bully more power.

Bystanders and colluders

Someone who sees a bullying incident take place is a 'bystander'. Even if a bystander doesn't join in, he or she is still involved, because they are there when the bullying happens. A bystander who does nothing is in fact approving of the bullying — he or she is a 'colluder'.

Get involved

Some people think that bullying is only an issue for bullies and their victims, but others think bullying involves everyone who knows it is taking place. Here are some ways for a bystander to stop a bullying incident:

• Go and tell an adult.
• Show that you disapprove of what you are seeing.
• If it is safe, tell the bully to stop.
• Go and get the help of your friends to come together and tell the bully to stop.
• Become friends with the person who is being bullied.
• Encourage the bullied person to tell an adult about the bullying.

Someone who sees bullying happen is a bystander. If they do nothing about it, they are a colluder.

YOUR CALL Your friends are bullying a boy in your class. You don't like what you have seen your friends do, and you don't join in. But you don't tell on them either. The boy names you as one of the bullies. Is this fair?

FOR!

AGAINST!

- Bullying is wrong, and should never be kept secret.
- When you tell on a bully, you stop something bad from happening.

- If you tell on a bully, next time they might pick on you.
- People should learn to stand up for themselves.

Making friends with someone who is being bullied can bring the bullying to a halt.

ROLE-PLAY: KEEP OUT OF TROUBLE...

These children disagree about bullying. Who is right?

1 "Kids who watch the leader of their gang pick on someone, but don't do anything to stop it are bullies too."

Victim of bullying, Azi Fagbemi

2 "If your mate's bullying someone, it's better to let him get on with it, or he may start picking on you."

School gang member, Dean Tucker

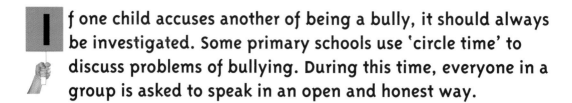

Anti-bullying groups

If one child accuses another of being a bully, it should always be investigated. Some primary schools use 'circle time' to discuss problems of bullying. During this time, everyone in a group is asked to speak in an open and honest way.

Anti-bullying policies

Most schools have anti-bullying policies. These explain what pupils and parents should do in cases of bullying, and say what the school will do to solve a problem. In the UK, schools are allowed to take action against bullying behaviour on the journey to and from school.

School councils

Many schools set up councils for children to discuss issues like bullying. Some people believe school councils help a school to tackle bullying. Others believe that school councils don't have any real influence over how schools are run.

A headteacher discusses an accusation of bullying with a pupil. Most schools take accusations of bullying very seriously.

Many schools encourage children to speak out about bullying, for example during 'circle time'.

? Dilemma:

Layla was in the gang that bullied Amy, but she didn't actually hurt her. Now everyone thinks she is a bully. What should she do in future?

IN FOCUS

Bullying support groups

Help and advice about bullying doesn't only exist in schools. There are useful telephone helplines and online support groups, such as Childline. These are run by trained experts. Anyone can contact a bullying support group — someone who is bullied, knows someone who is, or is a bully themselves.

Pupil support

In some schools, pupils are trained to talk to bullies and their victims. They learn how to help sort out problems, and to discover why bullying happened in the first place. This is called peer support or peer mediation (see page 20).

YOUR CALL Do you think children should take on peer support roles, or should this kind of work be left to adults?

Glossary

Abuse	Unpleasant and harmful behaviour towards somebody.
Actual bodily harm	Injuries caused by a physical attack.
Autism	A mental condition which makes it hard to communicate with other people.
Bystander	Someone who sees another person being bullied.
Chat room	A place on the Internet where people can communicate with each other by typing messages on their computer.
Colluder	Someone who sees another person being bullied, but does nothing about it.
Criminal record	A list of crimes for which a person has been convicted.
Cyber bullying	Bullying that happens on the Internet or mobile phones.
Depression	A sad state of mind which takes away a person's energy and makes it hard for them to concentrate on anything.
Dyslexia	A learning difficulty that makes it hard for a person to read, write and spell.
Emotional bullying	A kind of bullying that makes a person feel sad, upset and left out.
Graffiti	Words or drawings scribbled on a wall.
Happy slapping	Physical bullying that is filmed on a mobile phone and sent to other people.
Helpline	A phone number that people can call to get help with their problems.
Homophobic	Prejudiced against people who are homosexual (gay).
Martial arts	Styles of fighting from the Far East, for example judo and karate, which can be used for self-defence.
Obesity	The condition of being very overweight.
Online	Connected to the Internet.
Peer group	A group of people who are equal in age or importance.
Physical bullying	A kind of bullying that causes physical harm or damage.
Pin code	A combination of numbers known only by you, that gives you access to something private.
Prejudice	An opinion about something that is not based on facts.
Racism	Treating someone unfairly because they are from a different race, country, culture or religion.
Rumour	Something which lots of people are saying, which may not be true.
Self-esteem	How you feel about yourself.
Sibling	A brother or sister.
Suicide	The act of killing yourself.
Support group	A group that gives help and advice to people with problems.
Verbal bullying	A kind of bullying that involves words, either spoken or written down.
Witness	Someone who sees something.

Further information

Websites

United Kingdom
www.bullying.co.uk
www.antibullying.net
www.beatbullying.org

Three excellent UK-based websites, which each give helpful information and offer support for children and adults on the subject of bullying.

www.childline.org.uk

A very good children's website that is run by the UK children's charity, the NSPCC. The website gives information about a range of issues affecting children, including bullying. The helpline gives confidential advice and support to children who have a problem and need to talk about it.

www.nspcc.org.uk

A children's charity that campaigns to stop child abuse. The website has helpful information about bullying, and useful educational resources.

www.kidscape.org.uk

A UK charity aimed at preventing bullying and child abuse. The website has a useful advice section for children and parents on the subject of bullying.

United States
www.stopbullyingnow.hrsa.org

An excellent website for children, with information, help and advice about bullying. The website has games to play on, and there is a section in the Spanish language.

Australia
www.bullyingnoway.com.au

A very good Australian website aimed at children, parents and teachers. The website offers a variety of information, ideas and resources on the issue of bullying.

New Zealand
www.beyondbullying.co.nz

A New Zealand-based website that gives general information about bullying, with a particular focus on bullying that takes place between adults in the workplace.

Note to parents and teachers: Every effort has been made by the Publishers to ensure that these websites are suitable for children, that they are of the highest educational value, and that they contain no inappropriate or offensive material. However, because of the nature of the Internet, it is impossible to guarantee that the contents of these sites will not be altered. We strongly advise that Internet access is supervised by a responsible adult.

Index

These are the lists of contents for each title in *Your Call:*

Alcohol
What is alcohol? • What happens when you drink alcohol? • Alcohol in everyday life • Social drinking • Learning to drink • Under-age drinking • Binge drinking • Alcohol and health • Addicted to alcohol • Alcohol and the law • Drink-driving • Alcohol and violence • Alcohol in different cultures

Animal Rights
About animal rights • Eating animals • Wearing fur • Farm animals • Hunting and fishing • Culling • Working animals • Sporting and circus animals • Zoos and safari parks • Pets • Animal research • Breeding and pedigree • Endangered animals

Being A Vegetarian
What is a vegetarian? • What is a vegan? • Animal welfare • Green vegetarians • Feeding the world • The healthy choice? • A balanced diet Vegetarian children • Read the label • Going vegetarian • Clothes and make-up • Extreme vegetarians • Vegetarianism around the world

Bullying
What is bullying? • Why do people bully? • Emotional bullying • Verbal bullying • Physical bullying • Cyber bullying • Racist bullying • Bullying at home • Bullying at school • Bullying in sport • Stop the bullying! • Being a witness • Anti-bullying groups

Campaigning for Change
Why do people campaign for change? • Lobbying and pressure groups • Demonstrations, marches and rallies • Publicity stunts • Big events • Charities • Media campaigns • Local campaigns • Raising awareness • Campaign labels and marks • Modern technology • Extremists • Getting involved

Gangs
About gangs • Why people join gangs • Looking alike • Group behaviour • Peaceful gangs • Violent gangs • Girl gangs • Turf wars • Knife crimes • Gun crimes • Social crimes • Safer streets • Youth projects